by John Updike

TOSSING
and
TURNING

John Updike

TOSSING
and
TURNING

POEMS

Alfred A. Knopf · New York
1977

THIS IS A BORZOI BOOK
PUBLISHED BY ALFRED A. KNOPF, INC.

Published in the United States by Alfred A. Knopf, Inc., New York, and simultaneously in Canada by Random House of Canada Limited, Toronto. Distributed by Random House, Inc., New York.

Grateful acknowledgment is made to Random House, Inc., for permission to reprint the quotation from *Ulysses* by James Joyce. Copyright 1914, 1918 by James Joyce and renewed 1942, 1946 by Nora Joseph Joyce.

Library of Congress Cataloging in Publication Data
Updike, John.
Tossing and turning.
I. Title.
PS3571.P4A17   1977   811'.5'4   76-44002
ISBN 0-394-41090-4

Manufactured in the United States of America
First Edition

6.15.77 Ingram 4.77

ACKNOWLEDGMENTS

Some of these poems were previously published in *The New Republic, Harper's Magazine, The Atlantic Monthly, The American Scholar, Commonweal, Bits, Quest Magazine, The Boston Review of the Arts, Boston University Journal, Harvard Bulletin, New York Quarterly, Punch, Polymus, Crazy Horse, Transatlantic Review, Paris Review, Saturday Review* and *Ontario Review.* The following poems first appeared in *The New Yorker:* "The House Growing," "The Cars in Caracas," "Upon Shaving Off One's Beard," "Insomnia the Gem of the Ocean," "A Bicycle Chain," "Mime," "Phenomena," "Heading for Nandi," "Dream and Reality," and "Calder's Hands." "Bath After Sailing," "Sunday in Boston," and "Query" were published in small editions by Country Squires Books (Stevenson, Connecticut), Rook Broadsides (Pittsburgh, Pennsylvania) and Albondocani Press (New York) respectively; "Cunts" and six of the shorter poems (as *Six Poems*) were issued in book form by Frank Hallman of New York. Grateful acknowledgment is also made to Miguel Otera Silva and *El Nacional* for permission to reprint "Los Carros en Caracas."

to Martha

When first he saw. Alas!
Full tup. Full throb.
Warbling. Ah, lure! Alluring.
Martha! Come!
Clapclop. Clipclap. Clappyclap.
                    —*Ulysses*

CONTENTS

I

CONTENTS

CONTENTS

xi

I

YOU WHO SWIM

You who in water move as one
long rounded to this use, a stone
that gently fails to sink, you tint
as wind tints air this element.

Androgynous, your round face shorn
by bathing-cap, you feign to drown.
"The dead man's float" you say and smile,
your lashes wet and animal.

Soft teacher, otter, other, moth
to the sunk sun, you play at death;
the surface glitter slips, and air
slices your throat with shards of glare.

At night you rise beside me, face
wet with the dark, your dim lips spaced
to hold the bubble love; your eyes
are shut. We swim our dead men's lives.

DREAM AND REALITY

I am in a room.
Everything is white, the walls
are white, there are no windows.
There is a door.
I open it, and neatly
as a shadow a coating of snow
falls door-shaped into the room.
I think, *Snow*, not surprised
it is inside and outside both,
as with an igloo.
I move through the open door
into the next room; this, too, is
white and windowless and perfect.
I think, *There must be more than this.*
This is a dream.

My daughter finds bones
on the marshes. I examine them:
deer heads with sockets round as
cartoon eyes, slender jaws broken.
There are tiny things too,
no bigger than a pulled tooth,
and just that white—burs of bone,
intricate, with pricking flanges
where miniature muscles attached.
She says, *Those are mouse jaws.*
Indeed: I see teeth like rows

of the letter "i" in diamond type.
She tells me, *I find them*
in the cough balls of owls.
And this is reality.

THE SOLITARY POND

The fall we moved to the farm, I was thirteen;
the half-wild grapes on the dilapidated arbor
could not be eaten, and the forests and brown fields
also seemed to have no purpose. I grew accustomed,

that winter before the first spring, to hike alone,
ducking first under our barbed wire, then our neighbor's,
through thorny and hurricane-hit woods to a store
selling candy and soft drink and gas by Route 11.

Returning one afternoon along an old wall,
I came to a shallow, solitary pond, frozen,
not more than fifteen feet across, and lined with stalks
and briar-strands that left the center scarcely open.

Recalling the rink in the town we had moved from,
I fetched my dull skates from the attic chest and
    blundered
back through sharp thickets while the cold grew and a
    frown
from the sky deepened the ominous area under

the black branches. My fingers were numb at the laces,
and the ice was riddled with twigs, and my intent
to glide back to childhood absurd. I fell, unstable
on the clutter of wood and water bubbled and bent
like earth itself, and thrashed home through the trees
    hating
the very scratches left by my experiment.

LEAVING CHURCH EARLY

What, I wonder, were we hurrying to,
my grandfather, father, mother, myself,
as the last anthem was commencing? Were
we avoiding the minister's hand at the door?
My mother shied, in summer, from being touched.
Or was it my father, who thought life was grim
and music superfluous, dodging the final hymn?
Or could, I wonder now, the impetus
that moved the small procession of us up
and out, apologizing, from the pew
have come from the ancient man, mysterious
to me as an ancestor turned to ash,
who held some thunders though, a village bully
in his time and still a steadfast disliker
of other people's voices? Whatever the cause,
we moved, *bump* and whisper, down
the side aisle, while the organ mulled Stanza One,
a quadruped herd, branded as kin, I
the last of the line, adolescent, a-blush,
out through the odor of piety and the scents
(some purchased at Kresge's, some given by God)
my buxom country cousins harbored in
their cotton dresses, to the sighing exit
which opened on the upbeat as the choir
in love of the Lord and imperfect unison
flung its best self over the balcony.

The lifted voices drifted behind us, absurd.
Loose pebbles acknowledged our shoes.
Our Buick, black and '36, was parked

in a hickory picnic grove where a quoit stake,
invisible as Satan in the grass
of Eden, might spear a tire "of the unwary,"
as my grandfather put it. The interior
of the auto hit us with an hour's heat.
We got in gear, our good clothes mussed,
and, exonerated for the week, bounced home.

Home: the fields, red, with acid rows of corn
and sandstone corner-markers. The undertone
of insect-hum, the birds too full to sing.
A Sunday haze in Pennsylvania.
My unchurched grandma caught in the foursquare house,
as we prattled in the door, like a burglar
trapped in mid-theft, half-paralyzed, her frame
hung in my memory between two tasks,
about to do something, but what? A cream
jug droops in her hand, empty or it would spill—
or is it a potato-masher, or
a wooden spoon? White-haired, stricken, she stares
and to welcome us back searches for a word.

What had we hurried back to? There could be
no work, a mock-Genesiac rest reigned
in the bewitched farmland. Our strawberries
rotted in their rows unrummaged-for;
No snorting, distant tractor underlined
the rasp of my father's pencil as he marked,
with his disappointed grimace, math exams.
The dogs smelled boredom, and collapsed.
The colors of the Sunday comics jangled,
printed off-key, and my grandfather's feet,
settling in for a soliloquy, kicked up fuzz.

My father stood to promenade his wounds.
I lay down, feeling weak, and pulled a book
across my eyes the way a Bedouin
waiting out a sandstorm drapes his sheet.
The women clucked and quarrelled with the pots
over who was cook. A foody fog
arose. The dogs rose with it, and the day
looked as if it might survive to noon.

What is wrong with this picture? What is strange?
Each figure tends its own direction, keeps
the axis of its own theatric chore,
scattered, anarchic, kept home by poverty,
with nowhere else to go. A modern tribe
would be aligned around "the television,"
the family show-off, the sparkling prodigy
that needs a constant watching lest it sulk and cease
to lift into celebrity the arc
of interlocked anonymous: we were not such.
We spurned all entertainment but our misery.
"Jesus," my father cried, "I hate the world!"
"Mother," my mother called, "you're in the way!"
"Be grateful for your blessings," Grandpa advised,
shifting his feet and showing a hairless shin.
"*Ach*," Grandma brought out in self-defense,
the syllable a gem of German indignation,
its guttural edge unchipped, while I,
still in the sabbath shirt and necktie, bent
my hopes into the latest Nero Wolfe, imagining
myself orchidaceous in Manhattan and
mentally constructing, not Whodunit,
but How to Get Out of Here: my dastardly plot.

The rug, my closest friend, ignored
my elbows. Geraniums raged on the sills.
The furniture formed a living dismal history
of heritage, abandonment, and purchase,
pretension, compromise, and wear: the books
tried to believe in a better world but failed.
An incongruous painting told of dunes
and a dab of unattainable sea.
Outside, a lone car passed, the mailbox held
no hope of visitation; no peacock magazine,
wrapped in brown paper, rife with ads, would come
to unremind us of what we were, poor souls
who had left church early to be about
the business of soaking ourselves in Time,
dunking doughnuts let fall into the cup.
Hot Pennsylvania, hazy, hugged the walls
of sandstone two feet thick as other cells
enfold the carcinomic hyperactive one; we were
diseased, unneighborly, five times alone, and quick.

What was our hurry? Sunday afternoon
beckoned with radioed ballgames, soft ice cream,
furtive trips into the county, naps
for the elderly, daydreams for the young,
while blind growth steamed to the horizon of hills,
the Lord ignoring His own injunction to rest.
My book grew faint. My grandfather lifted his head,
attentive to what he alone divined;
his glasses caught the light, his nose
reclaimed an ancient handsomeness.
His wife, wordless, came and sat beside.
My father swished his hips within his bath of humor

and called his latest recognition to the other
co-captain of dissatisfaction; my mother
came to the living-room doorway, and told us off.
She is the captive, we are the clumsy princes
who jammed the casket with our bitter kisses.
She is our prison, the rampart of her forehead
a fiery red. We shake our chains, amused.
Her myths and our enactment of them tickle better
the underside of facts than Bible fables;
here to this house, this mythy *then*, we hurried,
dodging the benediction to bestow,
ourselves upon ourselves, the blessing.

Envoi

My mother, only you remember with me,
you alone still populate that room.
You write me cheerful letters mentioning Cher
and Barbara Walters as if they were there with you,
realer than the dead. We left church early
why? To talk? To love? To eat? To be free
of cant not of our own patenting? You read,
you write me, Aristotle and Tolstoi
and claim to be amazed, how much they knew.
I send you this poem as my piece of the puzzle.
We know the truth of it, the past, how strange,
how many corners wouldn't bear describing,
the "rubbing elbows," how busy we were forgiving—
we had no time, of course, we *have* no time
to do all the forgiving that we must do.

THE HOUSE GROWING

April 1972

The old house grows, adding rooms of silence.
My grandfather coughing as if to uproot
burdock from his lungs,
my grandmother tapping a ragged path
from duty to duty, and now
my father, prancing and whinnying
to dramatize his battle for the dollar,
pricking himself with pens to start each day—
all silent. The house grows vast.
Its windows take bites of the sky
to feed its flight toward emptiness. The mantel
restates its curve of molding undismayed,
the hearthstones fatten on the vanished.

QUERY

Pear tree, why blossom?
Why push this hard glitter
of life from your corpse?

Headless and hollow,
each major limb broken
by old storm or snowfall,
you startle the spring.

Doesn't it hurt?
Your petals say not,
froth from your shell
like laughter, like breath.

But (your branchlets spew up
in an agony's
spoutings) it must.

LATE JANUARY

The elms' silhouettes
again relent,
leafless but furred

with the promise of leaves,
dull red in a sky dull yellow
with the threat of snow.

That blur, verging on growth:
Time's sharp edge is slitting
another envelope.

TOUCH OF SPRING

Thin wind winds off the water,
earth lies locked in dead snow,
but sun slants in under the yew hedge,
and the ground there is bare,
with some green blades there,
and my cat knows,
sharpening her claws on the flesh-pink wood.

MELTING

Airily ice congeals on high
from Earth's calm breath and slantwise falls
and six-armed holds its crystal faith until
Sun, remembering his lordly duty, burns.

Commences then this vast collection:
gutters, sewers, rivulets
relieve the finned drift's weight
and the pace-packed pavement unsheathe.

It glistens, drips, purls—the World:
brightness steaming, elixir sifting
by gravity's simplicity from all that will silt.

The round-mouthed drains, the square-mouthed grates
take, and they take; down tunnels runs
the dead storm sobbing, Proserpine.

BATH AFTER SAILING

From ten to five we whacked the waves,
the hostile, mobile black
that lurched beneath the leeward winch
as helplessly we heeled.

Now after six I lie at ease,
at ease in a saltless sea my size,
my fingertips shrivelled as if dead,
the sway of the sloop still haunting the tub.

I can't stop seeing the heartless waves
the mirthless color of green tar
sliding on themselves like ball-bearings,
deep and opaque and not me,

not me: I was afraid,
afraid of heeling over in the wind
and inhaling bubbling lead
and sinking, opaque as stone.

Lord, how light my feet,
wed to their salt-soaked sneakers,
felt on the dock, amid the mysterious
steadiness of trees and air.

I did not want, I had not wanted
to die. I saw death's face
in that mass absorbed
in shrugging off its timeless weight,

the same dull mass blond Vikings scanned,
impervious to all the sailor love
thrust onto it. My shredded hand
ached on the jib sheet line.

The boat would clumsily, broken
wings flapping, come about,
and the slickered skipper search
the sea-face and find me gone,

his surprise not total,
and one wave much like the rest,
a toppling ton, a rib of time,
an urgent message from nothing to nothing.

I thank you, God of trees and air,
whose steeples testify
to something steady slipped by chance
upon Your tar-green sliding face,

for this my mock survival.
My children's voices plumb my death.
My rippling legs are hydra limbs.
My penis, my representative,

my emissary to darkness, survivor
of many a plunge, flipflops
sideways, alive and small
and pallid in reprieve.

Black sea, deep sea, you dangle
beneath my bliss like a dreadful gamble.

Mute, white as a swimming pool cork,
I float on the skin

of sleepiness, of my sleep,
of all sleep . . . how much I prefer
this microcosmic version
of flirting with immersion.

ON AN ISLAND

Islanded, my wife turned on the radio for news of home.
Instead she heard that near us a plane had crashed into the
    sea.

She told me after dinner she couldn't face the flight home:
"What would I tell the children as we go down?"

I pooh-poohed her of course, told her the long odds;
we made love with a desperate undercurrent, and fell
    asleep.

Then I awoke in the dark, and her fears appeared real.
The blinds were tilted black, my sunburn hurt, I was
    thirsty.

The tranquil ocean was yet enormous in its noise;
mad hissing pursued me into each of the rooms.

My children were asleep, each small mouth darkly open;
"The radio said that a couple with a ten-year-old child

was found in the water, their bodies still clutching him."
Moonlight, pale as a moth, chasmed the front room with
    shadow

and lay white on the water, white on the sliding,
the huge-shushing sliding from island to island—

sleepless, inanimate, bottomless, prayer-denying,
the soughing of matter cast off by the sun, blind sun

among suns, massed liquid of atoms that conceives
and consumes, that communes with itself only,

soulless and mighty; our planes, our islands sink:
a still moon plates the sealed spot where they were.

WIND

If God has any voice it is the wind.

How women hate
this seeking of a vacuum;
it gets their edges up,
they cannot sleep, they think
of Boreas impregnating primeval Night,
of skirts rudely lifted in funhouses.

It is death made loud:
nowhereness bellowing,
now reedy along the copper eaves,
now ballooned to a manifold softness by a tree,
now scraping like flint on the surface of water,
making arrowhead wrinkles,
seeking somewhere to stop and be.

I lie here listening.
God is crying, *for-
giiiive*, demanding, *fore-
go-ooo*, proclaiming, *no-
wheerrre*, and begging,
let go-oo-ohhh.

In His mouth my body tastes like stale milk.

POISONED IN NASSAU

By the fourth (or is it the fifth?)
day, one feels poisoned—by
last night's rum, this morning's sun,
the tireless pressure of leisure.

The sea's pale green seems evil.
The shells seem pellets, the meals
forced doses, Bahamian cooking
as bitterly obsequious as
the resentful wraiths that serve it.

Vertigo is reading at the beach
words a thousand miles away,
is tasting Coppertone again,
is closing one's eyes once more against
the mismatch of poverty and beauty.

The beautiful sea is pale, it is
sick, its fish sting like regrets.
Perhaps it was the conch salad, or is
the something too rich in Creation.

RAINING IN MAGENS BAY

The sky, paid to be blue,
yields at most patches of silver
and then, salted with sun, rain
(we can't quite believe it)
so heavy the branches of sea-grape
give no shelter. Run!

The towel, the book, the sunglasses:
save them, and save our fair skins
from the pelting,
bitter and chill, that dyes the arms
of the bay the color of smoke
and erases Outer Brass Island.

Wait, there is a way,
a way not to panic. The picnic
by the cabaña has not stopped cackling;
its voices ricochet louder,
wind-whipped, from lips
an inch above the skin of water.

They have gone swimming,
and the lovers up the beach
persist in embracing submerged.
Come, the calm green is alive
with drops, and soft; one's shadow
no longer lurks below like a shark.

The way to get out of the rain

is to get into the water.
The way for rain to fall
is mixed with sun, like salt.
The way for man to be is mixed
with sun and salt and sea and shadow.

SLEEPLESS IN SCARSDALE

Prosperity has stolen stupor from me.
The terraced lawn beneath my window
has drained off fatigue; the alertness
of the happy seizes me like rage.

Downstairs, the furniture matches.
The husband and wife are in love.
One son at Yale, another in law,
a third bowls them over in high school.

I rejoice. The bed is narrow.
I long for squalor's relaxation,
fantasizing a dirty scene
and mopping the sheet with a hanky.

There is a tension here. The books
look arranged. The bathroom
has towels of too many sizes.
I weigh myself on the scales.

Somewhere, a step. Muffled.
The stairs are carpeted.
A burglar has found us. A son
is drunk. The wife desires me.

But nothing happens, not even
oblivion. Life can be too clean.
Success like a screeching of brakes
pollutes the tunnel of silence.

Mock-Tudor, the houses are dark.
Even these decent trees sleep.
I await the hours guiltily,
hoping for one with whom I can make a deal.

SUNDAY IN BOSTON

The fags and their gay dogs are patrolling
the Garden; on Boylston the blacks,
hollow-backed, demonstrate styles of meander
in this hearttown theirs by default.

The winos on Commonwealth, wiser than wisdom,
blink eyes as pale as bottle bottoms;
sun-pickled, their faces, lined fine as maps,
beam from within this particular nowhere.

Pistachio George sits high. July beds bloom.
The Ritz's doorman sports his worn maroon.
Above us like a nearer sky great Pei's
glass sheet, cerulean, clasps clouds to its chest.

And, unapologetic in their pallor, girls
in jigging halters and sordid shorts parade
festive colorless flesh regathered from
its Saturday spill, the bearded lover split.

Brick Boston, city of students and drunks!
In Godless, doggy righteousness we bask.
The suburbs send us their stifling cars, and we
in turn give back the hollow sound of bells.

APOLOGIES TO HARVARD

The Phi Beta Kappa Poem, 1973

Dear, drear Harvard, crown of the pilgrim mind;
Home of the hermit scholar, who pursues
His variorums undistracted by
All riots, sensual or for a cause;
Vast village where the wise enjoy the young;
Refuge of the misshapen and unformed;
Stylistic medley (Richardson's stout brown,
Colonial scumble, Puseyite cement,
And robber-baron Gothic pile their slates
In floating soot, beneath house-tower domes
The playtime polychrome of M & Ms);
Fostering mother: Time that doth dissolve
Granite like soap and dries to bone all tears
Devoured my quartet of student years
And, stranger still, the twenty minus one
Since I was hatched and certified your son.

A generation steeped in speed and song,
In Doctor Spock, TV, and denim *chic*
Has come and gone since, Harvard, we swapped vows
And kept them—mine, to grease the bursar's palm,
To double-space submitted work, to fill
All bluebooks set before me (spilling ink
As avidly as puppies lap a bowl
Till empty of the blankness of the milk),
To wear a tie and jacket to my meals,

To drop no water bags from windows, nor
Myself (though *Werther*, Kierkegaard, and *Lear*
All sang the blues, the deans did not, and warned
That suicide would constitute a blot
Upon one's record), to obey the rules
Yclept "parietal" (as if the walls, not I,
Were guilty if a girl were pinched between
Them after ten); in short, to strive, to bear,
To memorize my notes, to graduate:
Thus were my vows. Yours were, in gourmet terms,
To take me in, raw as I was, and chew
And chew and chew for one quadrennium,
And spit me out, by God, a gentleman.
We did our bits. All square, and no regrets.
On my side, little gratitude; but why?
So many other men—the founding race
Of farmer-divines, the budding Brahmins
Of Longfellow's time, the fragile sprats
Of fortunes spun on sweatshop spindles
Along the Merrimack, the golden crew
Of raccoon-coated hip-flask-swiggers and
Ritz-tea-dance goers, the continual tribe
Of the studious, the smart, and the shy—
Had left their love like mortar 'twixt your bricks,
Like sunlight synthesized within your leaves,
Had made your morning high noon of their days
And clung, there seemed no need for me to stay.
I came and paid, a trick, and stole away.

The Fifties—Cold-War years *par excellence*—
Loom in memory's mists as an iceberg, slow
In motion and sullenly radiant.

I think, those years, it often snowed because
My freshman melancholy took the print
Of a tread-marked boot in slush, crossing to Latin
Under Cerberean Dr. Havelock
In Sever 2, or to Lamont's Math 1
With some tall nameless blameless section man
To whom the elegant was obvious,
Who hung Greek letters on his blackboard curves
Like trinkets on a Christmas tree and who
I hope is happy in Schenectady,
Tending toward zero, with children my age then
To squint confused into his lucent mind.
There was a taste of coffee and of cold.
My parents' house had been a hothouse world
Of complicating, inward-feeding jokes.
Here, wit belonged to the dead; the wintry smiles
Of snowmen named Descartes and Marx and Milton
Hung moonlit in the blizzards of our brains.
Homesick, I walked to class with eyes downcast
On heelprints numberless as days to go.

And when bliss came, as it must to sophomores,
Snow toppled still, but evening-tinted mauve,
Exploding on the windows of the Fogg
Like implorations of a god locked out
While we were sealed secure inside, in love.
"In love"—not quite, but close enough, we felt,
To make a life or not, as chances willed.
Meanwhile there were cathedral fronts to know
And cigarettes to share—our breaths straight smoke—
And your bicycle, snickering, to wheel
Along the wet diagonal of the walk

That led Radcliffewards through the snowy Yard.
Kiss, kiss, the flakes surprised our faces; *oh,*
The arching branches overhead exclaimed,
Gray lost in gray like limestone ribs at Rheims;
Wow-ow!—as in a comic-strip balloon
A siren overstated its alarm,
Bent red around a corner hurtling toward
Extragalactic woe, and left behind
Our blue deserted world of silent storm.
Kikítta-kíkittá, your bike spokes spake
Well-manneredly, not wishing to impose
Their half-demented repetitious thoughts
Upon your voice, or mine: what *did* we say?
Your voice was like your skin, an immanence,
A latent tangency that swelled my cells,
Young giant deafened by my whirling size.
And in your room—brave girl, you had a room,
You were a woman, with inner space to fill,
Leased above Sparks Street, higher than a cloud—
Water whistled itself to tea, cups clicked,
Your flaxen flat-mate's quick Chicago voice
Incited us to word games, someone typed,
The telephone and radio checked in
With bulletins, and, nicest noise of all,
All noises died, the snow kept silent watch,
The slanting backroom private as a tent
Resounded with the rustle of our blood,
The susurration of surrendered clothes.

We took the world as given. Cigarettes
Were twenty-several cents a pack, and gas
As much per gallon. Sex came wrapped in rubber

And veiled in supernatural scruples—call
Them chivalry. A certain breathlessness
Was felt; perhaps the Bomb, which after all
Went *mu*SHROOM! as we entered puberty,
Waking us from the newspaper-nightmare
Our childhoods had napped through, was realer then;
Our lives, at least, were not assumed to be
Our right; we lived, by shifts, on sufferance.
The world contained policemen, true, and these
Should be avoided. Governments were bunk,
But well-intentioned. Blacks were beautiful
But seldom met. The poor were with ye always.
We thought one war as moral as the next,
Believed that life was tragic and absurd,
And were absurdly cheerful, just like Sartre.
We loved John Donne and Hopkins, Yeats and Pound,
Plus all things convolute and dry and pure.
Medieval history was rather swank;
Psychology was in the mind; abstract
Things grabbed us where we lived; the only life
Worth living was the private life; and—last,
Worst scandal in this characterization—
We did not know we were a generation.

Forgive us, Harvard; Royce and William James
Could not construe a Heaven we could reach.
We went forth, married blind, and bred like mink.
We seized what jobs the System offered, raked
Our front yards, sublimated for the kids,
And chalked up meekly as a rail-stock-holder
Each year's depreciation of our teeth,
Our skin-tone, hair, and confidence. The white

Of Truman's smile and Eisenhower's brow
Like mildew furs our hearts. The possible
Is but a suburb, Harvard, of your city.
Seniors, come forth; we crave your wrath and pity.

COMMENCEMENT, PINGREE SCHOOL

Among these North Shore tennis tans I sit,
In seersucker dressed, in small things fit;
Within a lovely tent of white I wait
To see my lovely daughter graduate.

Slim boughs of blossom tap the tent and stamp
    Their shadows like a bower on the cloth.
The brides in twos glide down the grassy ramp
    To graduation's candle, moth and moth.

The Master makes his harrumphs. Music. Prayer.
    Demure and close in rows, the seniors sway.
Class loyalty solidifies the air.
    At every name, a body wends her way

Through greenhouse shade and rustle to receive
A paper of divorce and endless leave.
As each accepts her scroll of rhetoric,
Up pops a Daddy with a Nikon. *Click.*

A L'ECOLE BERLITZ

Mademoiselle Printemps, my sometimes instructress,
with whom I slowly form pained sentences,
(*Je n'y en ai pas vu,*
par exemple, ou
A quelle heure vous êtes-vous couchée hier soir?)
at the end of one lesson
let down her French, and we faced
each other naked, I stripped
of the strange tongue that stiffly cloaks
each cretin utterance in dignity,
and she exposed in all her English vowels,
as luminous and slow as skin,
her consonants curling like bits of fleece,
the sense of her sentence as stunning and clear
as a tear-filled surrender.
"I am interested in doing translation,"
she said, and I couldn't think of a word. Not one.

SOUTH OF THE ALPS

Signorina Angeli, veteran of *Vogue*
and a New York marriage, had a heavy foot
between Milan and Como.
                    The speedometer swung
to 160 kilometers per hour,
pressed through trembling, and clung
like a locust husk that cannot let go.

    Presto, troppo presto!
the sides of our lemon Citroën hissed
at aquavita trucks we narrowly missed.
Less fluidly, in middle distance, villages
in red hats slowly turned to gaze
like groups of streetcorner pensioners
who had seen worse ruins than ours.
Green Alps, bearing aqueducts,
    drew dreamily near,
    a *quattrocento* paradise
extending its wings to bear us away.

Her chatting lover occupied the death seat. As
I cringed behind him, I felt my face
on the edge of explosion, my tender teeth
strewn in a stew of glass, my spine
a row of dominoes, my ghostless flesh
an interval of metal; and I saw her eyes
suspended in the rearview mirror,

immaculately calm:
                                   fringed jewels flattered
by the velvet hypnosis of her task.

       She was an ikon nailed
to the blank wall of our blinding speed:
her nose stiletto-straight, her nostrils
nice as a skull's, her lips downdrawn
upon the candy of her pout—
reversed details that linked
in clever foldout to the real:
to the empress oval of her tight-pulled hair,
her ear's pearl curve, her hands
at rest, with tips of nacre, on the wheel.

Beauty, deep in hock to time,
is reckless with its assets; I,
a cowardly word-hoarder, hugged my wish
to smudge more proofs with dubious
corrections. She was clean copy,
       her future a back issue.
Of course I adored her, though my fate
was a midge on her wrist she could twitch away;
the Old Testament said truly: fear
is love and love is rigid-making fear.

A traffic circle. The lake. We slowed.
Acknowledging my *grazie*, Signorina showed
on her smiling jaw a small mole *Vogue*
had airbrushed out.
                 Her mother—
who calls the Pope "Montini" and considers

him a Communist—had had the marriage annulled.
Hence, she is still "Signorina."

We ate, she, I, and her beau
   above Lake Como
   in green air so
soft we were not dizzy though
the lake was a little sky below,
the motorboats blunt comets.

   The wine
was Piedmontese and suave; the breeze
like a nerved-up gambler fidgeted with chips
of sunlight on the faded tablecloth.
   Bella, troppo bella.
Her hand fell heavy on my arm and grasped.
"Tell me—why doesn't anything last?"

CALDER'S HANDS

November 1976

In the little movie
at the Whitney
you can see them
at the center of the spell
of wire and metal:

a clumsy man's hands,
square and mitten-thick,
that do everything
without pause:
unroll a tiny rug

with a flick,
tug a doll's arm up,
separate threads:
these hands now dead
never doubted, never rested.

II

THE CARS IN CARACAS

The cars in Caracas
create a ruckukus,
a four-wheeled fracacas,
taxaxis and truckes.

Cacaphono-comic,
the tracaffic is farcic;
its weave leads the stomach
to turn Caracarsick.

The Venezuelan writer and political leader Miguel Otero
Silva returned this courtesy to his city with a translation into
Spanish:

LOS CARROS EN CARACAS

Los carros en Caracas
sufren de patatuses;
chillan sus matracas
taxaxis y busbuses.

Cacófono-estrambótico
el tráfico es traumático;
y te estruja el estómago
su oleaje caracásico.

BUSINESS ACQUAINTANCES

They intimately know just how our fortune lies
And share the murmured code of mutual enterprise,
So when we meet at parties, like lovers out of bed,
We blush to know that nothing real is being said.

UPON SHAVING OFF
ONE'S BEARD

The scissors cut the long-grown hair;
The razor scrapes the remnant fuzz.
Small-jawed, weak-chinned, big-eyed, I stare
At the forgotten boy I was.

INSOMNIA THE GEM
OF THE OCEAN

When I lay me down to sleep
My waterbed says, "Gurgle gleep,"
And when I readjustment crave
It answers with a tidal wave
That lifts me like a bark canoe
Adrift in breakers off Peru.

Neap to my spring, ebb to my flow,
It turns my pulse to undertow,
It turns my thoughts to bubbles, it
Still undulates when I would quit;
Two bags of water, it and I
In restless sympathy here lie.

TO A WATERBED

No Frog Prince ever had a pond
So faithful, murmurous, and fond.
Amniotically it sings
Of broken dreams and hidden springs,
Automatically it laves
My mind in secondary waves
That answer motions of my own,
However mild—my amnion.
Fond underbubble, warm and deep,
I love you so much I can't sleep.

COURTESY CALL

We again thank you for your esteemed order and
now wish to advise you that the clothes are awaiting
the pleasure of your visit.

—card from a London tailor

My clothes leaped up when I came in;
    My trousers cried, "Oh is it
Our own, our prince?" and split their pleats
    At the pleasure of my visit.

My jacket tried to dance with joy
    But lacked the legs; it screamed,
"Though our confusion is deplored,
    Your order is esteemed!"

"Dear clothes," I cooed, "at ease. Down, please.
    Adjust your warp and weft."
Said they, "We love you." I: "I know,
    I was advised," and left.

THE JOLLY GREENE GIANT

Or is it more shocking . . . to be forced to consider
that he may now be the largest of living English
novelists?—Greene, the ambidextrous producer of
"novels" and "entertainments"?
                        —*Reynolds Price, in* The New York Times
                                        Book Review

"You are large, Father Graham," the young fan opined,
    "And your corpus is bulky indeed;
Yet you pen 'entertainments' as thin as a rind—
    How do you so hugely succeed?"

"In my youth," said the writer, "I fasted on bile
    With lacings of Romanish rum;
Compounded each quarter, it swells all the while—
    Permit me to offer you some."

"Do you find," said the lad, "your gargantuan girth
    Impairs your professional finesse?
An author must calibrate Heaven and Earth
    To an eighth of an inch, I would guess."

"It is true," said the sage, "that my typing is rough,
    Though each key is as wide as a platter;
But the swattable critics hum wonderful stuff,
    And that is the heart of the matter!"

AUTHORS' RESIDENCES

After Visiting Hartford

Mark Twain's opinion was, he was entitled
  To live in style; his domicile entailed
Some seven servants, nineteen rooms, unbridled
      Fantasies by Tiffany
      That furnished hospitality
  With tons of stuff, until the funding failed.

The poet Wallace Stevens, less flamboyant,
  Resided in a whiter Hartford home,
As solid as his neighbors', slated, *voyant*
      For all its screening shrubs; from here
      He strolled to work, his life's plain beer
  Topped up with Fancy's iridescent foam.

And I, I live (as if you care) in chambers
  That number two—in one I sleep, alone
Most nights, and in the other drudge; my labors
      Have brought me to a little space
      In Boston. Writers, know your place
  Before it gets too modest to be known.

PAINTED WIVES

Soot, housedust, and tar didn't go far
With implacably bathing Madame Bonnard;
Her yellowish skin has immortally been
Turned mauve by the tints she was seen floating in.

Prim, pensive, and wan, Madame Cézanne
Posed with her purple-ish clothes oddly on;
Tipped slightly askew, and outlined in blue,
She seems to be hearing, "Stop moving, damn you!"

All lilac and cream and pink self-esteem,
Sweet Madame Renoir made sheer daylight dream;
In boas of air, without underwear,
She smiles through the brushstrokes at someone still there.

MILADY REFLECTS

RADIO SIGNALS BOUNCED OFF VENUS
—*Headline in* The New York Times

When I was known as Aphrodite, men
  Were wont to bounce their prayers off my side.
  I shrugged, and granted some, and some denied,
And even slept with mortals now and then.

But then Jehovah stormed in on a star
  And put a rapid end to such requests.
  "Well, cultures change," I thought; "the gods are guests
On Earth." I made the sky my sole boudoir.

Just yesterday, I felt an odd caress,
  A tickle or a whisper or a hum
  That smacked of Man—his opposable thumb,
His monkey face, his myths, his *humanness*.

Oh, dear. I'm not the girl he left alone.
  I have my books, my chocolates, and my maid—
  I know Mars thinks I've gotten rather staid.
I think I'll have them disconnect the phone.

SEVEN NEW WAYS OF LOOKING AT THE MOON

July 21, 1969

I

Man, am I sick
       of the moon.
We've turned it into one big
       television screen,
one more littered campsite,
one more high school yearbook
       signed, "Lots of luck,
              Richard Nixon."

II

Still, seeing Armstrong's strong leg
float down in creepy silhouette
       that first stark second
       was worth sitting up for.
Then it got too real, and seemed
       a George Pal Puppettoon
       called "Men on the Moon,"
mocked up on a Ping-Pong table.

III

Never again will I think of Houston
as full of rich men in cowboy hats:
       it is full

of numbers that like to talk
      and cajole.
They say, "Neil, start gathering rocks now"
and, "Buzz, about time to get back into
      your module."

IV

And how about little Luna
      snooping around
like a rusty private eye
      casing the motel
where we'd set up the tryst?

V

There was a backyard something
      that happened after
they put up the flag and laid out
the solar tinfoil and dug some holes.
      I had been there before,
playing marbles under a line of wash,
skinning my knees on the lack of grass.

VI

Since St. Paul filed his bulletins
standing headlines have been claiming
      SECOND COMING.
Now the type was broken up and used:
      MOON SEDUCING,
one "c" turned sideways as a "u".
Since no one came, we went.

VII

Well, I don't know. The media
have swamped the message, but anyway
     God bless the men.
     I loved the way they ran,
like bear-foot ghosts let out of school to say
that Death is probably O.K.
if all it means is being in the sky.
     Which answers why.

SKYEY DEVELOPMENTS

The clouds within the Milky Way
May well be diamonds, proudly say
Astronomers at U. of C.
The atmospheres of two or three
"Cool stars" could concentrate and freeze
More ice than winks at Tiffany's.

The pulsars, lately found to beep
Six times or so a sec., still keep
Themselves invisible, but are,
Perhaps, a kind of neutron star
So dense a cubic inch would tip
The scales against a battleship.

The moon, the men who jumped it swear,
Is like a spheric sandbox where
A child has dabbled; gray and black
Were all the colors they brought back.
The mad things dreamt of in the sky
Discomfort our philosophy.

NEWS FROM THE
UNDERWORLD

(After Blinking One's Way Through
"The Detection of Neutral Weak Currents,"
in Scientific American)

They haven't found the W
wee particle for carrying
the so-called "weak force" yet, but you
can bet they'll find some odder thing.

Neutrinos make a muon when
a proton, comin' through the rye,
hits in a burst of hadrons; then
eureka! γ splits from π

and scintillation counters say
that here a neutral lepton swerved.
Though parity has had its day,
the thing called "strangeness" is preserved.

SIN CITY, D.C.

as of our bicentennial summer

Hays Says Ray Lies;
Gravel Denies
Gray Houseboat Orgy Tale;
Gardner Claims Being Male
No Safeguard Against
Congressional Concupiscence;
Ray Parlays Hays Lay
Into Paperback Runaway.

III

A BICYCLE CHAIN

Left lying in the grass,
                          unconnected to anything,
disjunct and rusted,
                          it becomes itself.
Dangled, it will stiffly dance,
                               parodying legs,
or curl upon itself in balky knots
                          nothing like string's.

Neither liquid nor rigid,
                          it returns its metal
to organic semi-looseness: consult
                               a snake's skeleton
in a museum case, or watch
                          a python's differential curve
parabolize in oozy increments
                          behind safe glass.

Think of Insecta
                scaffolded together,
of protein atoms
                lightninged into viral chains,
of language's linked lines.
                          The thing is weighty
with its ancient seedtime secret,
                          articulation.

THE MELANCHOLY OF
STORM WINDOWS

We touch them at the raw turns
of the year—November,
with its whipped trees and cellar sky,
and April, whose air
promises more than the earth
seems willing to yield.
They are unwieldy, of wood, and their panes
monotonously ask the same question—*Am I clean?*

No, the answer is.
They fit less well, we feel, each year.
But the weather lowers,
watery and wider than a tide,
and if a seam or leak of light shows, well,
nothing's perfect under Heaven.
Our mortal shell,
they used to call the body.

In need of paint, they heave
up from the cellar and back down again
like a species of cloud,
shedding a snow of flakes and grime.
They rotate heavy in our hands; the screwdriver
stiffly twirls; the Windex swipes evaporate
in air ominous of coming worse
or, at winter's end, of Easter entombment,
of cobwebbed storage among belittling ants
while the grasshopper world above basks.

Stacked, they savor of the crypt,
of the unvisitable nook
and the stinking pipe, irreparable.
In place, they merely mitigate
death's whisper at the margins,
the knifing chill that hisses how
the Great Outer cares not a pin for our skins
and the airtight hearts that tremble therein.

We too are warped each fall.
They resemble us, storm windows,
in being gaunt, in losing putty,
in height, transparency, fragility—
weak slabs, poor shields, dull clouds.
Ambiguous, we have no place
where we, once screwed, can say, *At last.*

THE GRIEF OF CAFETERIAS

Everyone sitting alone with a sorrow,
overcoats on. The ceiling was stamped
of tin and painted over and over.
The walls are newer, and never matched.
SALISBURY STEAK SPECIAL $1.65.
Afterwhiffs of Art Deco chrome,
and the space is as if the space
of the old grand railroad terminals
was cut up, boxcarred out, and re-used.
SOUP SALAD & SANDWICH $1.29.
Nobody much here. The happiness
of that at least—of vacancy, mopped.
Behind cased food, in Hopper light,
the servers attend to each other, forever.

RATS

A house has rotten places: cellar walls
where mud replaces mortar every rain,
the loosening board that begged for nails in vain,
the sawed-off stairs, and smelly nether halls
the rare repairman never looks behind
and if he did would, disconcerted, find
long spaces, lathed, where dead air grows a scum
of fuzz, and rubble deepens crumb by crumb.

Here they live. Hear them on their boulevards
beneath the attic flooring tread the shards
of panes from long ago, and Fiberglas
fallen to dust, and droppings, and dry clues
to crimes no longer news. The villains pass
with scrabbly traffic-noise; their avenues
run parallel to chambers of our own
where we pretend we're clean and all alone.

SAND DOLLAR

This disc, stelliferous,
survived the tide
to tell us some small creature
lived and died;
its convex delicacy
defies the void
that crushed a vanished
echinoid.

Stoop down, delighted;
hoard in your hand
this sand-colored coin
redeemed from the sand
and know, my young sudden
archaeologist,
that other modes of being
do exist.

Behold the horizon.
Vastness acts
the wastrel with
its artifacts.
The sea holds lives
as a dream holds clues;
what one realm spends
another can use.

TOSSING AND TURNING

The spirit has infinite facets, but the body
confiningly few sides.
                              There is the left,
the right, the back, the belly, and tempting
in-betweens, northeasts and northwests,
that tip the heart and soon pinch circulation
in one or another arm.
                              Yet we turn each time
with fresh hope, believing that sleep
will visit us here, descending like an angel
down the angle our flesh's sextant sets,
tilted toward that unreachable star
hung in the night between our eyebrows, whence
dreams and good luck flow.
                              Uncross
your ankles. Unclench your philosophy.
This bed was invented by others; know we go
to sleep less to rest than to participate
in the orthic twists of another world.
This churning is our journey.
                              It ends,
can only end, around a corner
we do not know
                    we are turning.

LIVING WITH A WIFE

for Mary

At the Piano

Barefoot in purple pants
and my ski sweater you
play the piano most seriously
Mozart fumbled with a grimace
the lamplight fumbling unfelt
in the down of your neck

Kind field from which my progeny
have fled to grow voices and fangs
you are an arena where art
like a badly killed bull swerves again

Your bare foot lifts
the lamplight pedals on
my house is half music
my wife holds no harm

In the Tub

You are a pond mirroring
pink clouds there is moss
where your white roots meet
when you lift your arm to shave
you are a younger kind of tree

Silver you rise from the lead
your swan arm seeks a towel
magic has taken place because
my Excalibur razor is dull
and the water would boil a man

Under the Sunlamp

Neuter your hair tugged back
harshly your face a shield
of greased copper less sexy
than a boy by Donatello
too bright to look at long
eyelids sealed in *Urfreude*
metal locked in blinding earth

During Menstruation

My house is on fire red
pain flickers on the walls wet
flame runs downstairs eggs
are hurled unripe from the furnace
and a frown hurts like smoke

Help I am sliding my cry
stands helpless as Galileo
at the side of moons revolving
of unwinding novae burning
flinging Tampax tubes of ash

All the While

Upstairs to my downstairs
echo to my silence
you walk through my veins shopping
and spin food from my sleep

I hear your small noises
you hide in closets without handles
and surprise me from the cellar
your foot-soles bright black

You slip in and out of beauty
and imply that nothing is wrong
Who sent you?
What is your assignment?

Though years sneak by like children
it stays as unaccountable
as the underpants set to soak
in the bowl
where I would scour my teeth

MARCHING THROUGH A NOVEL

Each morning my characters
        greet me with misty faces
willing, though chilled, to muster
        for another day's progress
through the dazzling quicksand,
        the marsh of blank paper.
With instant obedience
        they change clothes and mannerisms,
drop a speech impediment,
        develop a motive backwards
to suit the deed that's done.
        They extend skeletal arms
for the handcuffs of contrivance,
        slog through docilely
maneuvers of coincidence,
        look toward me hopefully,
their general and quartermaster,
        for a clearer face, a bigger heart.
I do what I can for them,
        but it is not enough.
Forward is my order,
        though their bandages unravel
and some have no backbones
        and some turn traitor
like heads with two faces
        and some fall forgotten
in the trenchwork of loose threads,
        poor puffs of cartoon flak.
Forward. Believe me, I love them
        though I march them to finish them off.

NIGHT FLIGHT, OVER OCEAN

Sweet fish tinned in the innocence of sleep,
we passengers parallel navigate
the firmament's subconscious-colored deep,
streaming aligned toward a landlocked gate.
Schooled (in customs, in foreign coin), from zone
to zone we slip, each clutching at the prize
(a camera, a seduction) torn from some lone
shore lost in our brain like the backs of our eyes.
Nationless, nowhere, we dream the ocean
we motionless plummet above, our roaring
discreet as a stewardess padding, stray yen
or shillings jingling in the sky of our snoring.
Incipient, we stir; we burgeon, blank
dim swimmers borne toward the touchdown spank.

GOLFERS

One-gloved beasts in cleats, they come clattering
down to the locker room in bogus triumph, bulls
with the *pics* of their pars still noisy in them,
breathing false fire of stride, strike, stride, and putt.
We dread them, their brown arms and rasp of money,
their slacks the colors of ice cream, their shoes
whiter than bones that stipple the downtrodden green,
that take an open stance on the backs of the poor.
Breathing of bourbon, crowing, they strip:
the hair of their chests is grizzled, their genitals
hang dead as practice balls, their blue legs twist;
where, now, are their pars and their furor?
Emerging from the shower shrunken, they are men,
mere men, old boys, lost, the last hole a horror.

PALE BLISS

Splitting a bottle of white wine
with a naked woman
in the middle of the day.

CUNTS

(Upon Receiving The Swingers Life Club
Membership Solicitation)

The Venus de Milo didn't have one, at least no pussy
that left its shadow in the marble, but Botticelli's Venus,
though we cannot see it for her sea-anemone hand,
did, no doubt—an amber-furred dear mouth we would kiss
could we enter the Arcadian plane of the painting.
We must assimilate cunts to our creed of beauty.
September Morn held her thighs tight shut, and the dolls
we grew up undressing had nothing much there, not even
        MADE IN USA,
but the beauties we must learn to worship now all
have spread legs, splayed in bedspreaded motel beds,
and the snowflakes that burst forth are no two alike:
convolute snapdragons, portals and tears
and T-bones of hair, lips lurid as slices of salmon,
whirlpooly wisps more ticklish than skin, black brooms
a witch could ride cackling through the spatter of stars,
assholes a-stare like monocles tiny as dimes.

"I adore french culture and can really blow your mind"
"half of an ultra-sophisticated couple who prefers"
"love modelling with guys or gals and groovy parties"
"affectionate young housewife would like to meet"
"attractive broadminded funloving exotic tastes"
glory Gloria fellatio Felicia Connie your cunt

is Platonism upside down and really opens innocence
the last inch wider: I bite and I believe.

"Who put this mouse between my legs if not the Lord?
Who knocks to enter? Pigs of many stripes.
My cunt is me, it lathers and it loves
because its emptiness knows nothing else to do.
Here comes the stalwart cock, numb-headed hater,
assassin dragging behind him in a wrinkled sack
reproduction's two stooges; refrigerated in blood,
the salt sperm thrashes to mix with my lipstick.
Nibble my nipples, you fish. My eyelashes tickle your
        glans
while my cunt like a shark gone senile yawns for its meal.
In my prison your head will lean against the wet red wall
and beg for a pardon and my blood will beat back No.
Here is my being, my jewel, simpler than a diamond,
finer-spun than Assyrian gold and the Book of Kells,
nobler than a theorem by Euler, more darling than a
        dimple
in a Steuben-glass Shirley Temple—flesh-flower, riddle
of more levels than a Pyramid passageway greased with
        balm.
Adore!"

        A woman once upon a bed with me
to kiss my soul went down but in addition thrust
her ass up to my face and trembled all her length
so I knew something rare was being served; of course
the lapping was an ecstasy, but such an ecstasy
I prayed her distant face grow still so I could drink

the deeper of this widening self that only lacked
the prick of stars to be a firmament.

                                   "Adore
this hole that bleeds with the moon so you can be born!"
Stretched like a howl between the feet pushing the stirrups
the poor slit yields up the bubble of a skull.
Glad tunnel of life, foretaste of resurrection,
slick applicant of appropriate friction
springing loose the critical honey from the delirious bee.

"You can meet these swinging gals" *"you*
can be in direct contact with these free-thinking modern
        people"
"if you are a polaroid photography enthusiast"
"you can rest assured your membership"
"you will discover the most exquisite, intimate"
"you"   and the clitoris
like a little hurt girl turns its face to the corner.

Well, how were we to know that all you fat sweethearts
were as much the vagina's victim as the poor satyr who
        sells
his mother's IBM preferred to procure three whores
to have three ways at once—by land, by sea, by air?
"It was all a sacred mush of little pips to me."
Now you tell us, tell us and tell us, of a magical doorbell
crocheted of swollen nerves beneath the fur
and all the pallid moon from scalp to toes decuple
not quite this molehill of a mountain is

the Mare of Disenchantment, the Plain of No Response.
Who could have known, when you are edible all over?
So edible we gobble even your political views
as they untwist in lamplight, like lemon peel from a knife.

Tell us O tell us why is it why
the hairs on the nape of your neck say cunt
and the swirl in your laugh says cunt
and your fingernails flanking your cigarette
and the red of the roof of your mouth and your mischief
and your passion for sleeping dogs and the way
you shape hamburgers naked-handed and the way
you squat to a crying child so the labia stain
your underpants cry cunt CUNT there is almost
CUNT too much of a CUNT good thing CUNT

"And howzabout
that split banana second when
(a clouded tear in its single eye,
stiff angel stuffed with ichor)
the semen in good faith leaps
(no shadows live on marble
like these that coat my helpless hands)
and your [unmentionable]
enhouses the cosmic stranger with a pinch?"

☞ It is true, something vital ebbs from the process
once the female is considered not a monstrous emissary
from the natural darkness but as possessing personhood
with its attendant rights, and wit.

I pulled a Tampax with my teeth and found it, darling,
not so bloody. I loved the death between your toes.

I gazed my sallow fill in motel light until
your cunt became my own, and I a girl. I lost
my hard-on quite; my consciousness stayed raised.
Your mouth became a fumble at my groin.
You would not let me buck away. I came,
and sobbed, triumphantly repentant. You said
with a smile of surprise it was warm,
warm on the back of your throat, hitting,
and not salty, but sweet.
We want to fill your cunt but are unmanned.
My sobbing felt like coming. Fond monster,
you swallowed my tears. We were plighted.
I was afraid. I adore your cunt. But why
is there only one? Is one enough? You *cunt.*

"I'm available . . . and so are hundreds of other
eager young girls who are ready to pose FOR YOU!"
Corinna, even your shit has something to be said for it
"avant garde of a new era of freedom" (Coronet)
"dawn of a cultural phenomenon" (Playboy)
"Dr. Gilbert Bartell, the renowned cultural
       anthropologist"
"page after page of totally rewarding sexual knowledge
that will be an invaluable asset in your search for greater
sexual understanding Only through complete
       understanding
can man hope" "Discretion is our middle name!"
Daphne, your fortune moistens. Stand. Bend down. Smile.

PUSSY

A Preliminary Epithalamium

Tendrilous cloudlet in nakedness's sheer sky:
welcome mat gathered where the flowing body forks
and makes known its crux: wave-crest upon the shoal
where exaltedness founders and foamingly sinks:
bull's-eye where even the absent-minded arrow home:

forest concealing the hunted that is itself:
lair and prey and predator at once, sly fur
and arcanum, fragrant of woodfern and mossmulch,
furtive in its underbrush, fine nerves alert
yet asleep in the fitness of whatever is heavenly made:

dark gown the cunt put on to go out walking upright
that then, redundantly, let itself be gowned
in underpants, dank girdles, G-strings, step-ins, slips
through whose weave your triangular blot like a
      watermark
shines in the minds of the masculine perusers:

remainder, reminder of all that is animal:
dregs at the V of the torso's white wineglass,
concentrate, essence, summary, footnote,
addendum that cancels, in Gothic black letter,
Platonic misreadings of the belly's bland text:

concealer of lips, like a mustache, netherly,
feathery, tentative, tendermost, utterly

underhand-holdable: grace, veil and tracer, mane,
vague mass, forbidding mask, dark witticism, witty touch,
Grail, doe's tail, shy signal, and mere mystery:

let man never weary of such doting denoting,
such cunnilocutions and lingual adoration.
See him rise from his knees, chin wet and abraded
but slavish heart in harmony: chords ring beyond
the muffled clitoris of which he is one note, but one

the music needs to smuggle itself from silence.
My saint, impose the jubilant penance whereby
the gateways to rest batter down: absolve my rod.
Your pussy, it is my pet, it is my altar, *totaliter
aliter:* unknowable, known, and wild, subdued.

SUNDAY

This day that would tell us what we are
    if we would but listen
this day that is all gray sea
   with no bell buoys to ring the changes
     or turn us toward an appointed shore

into our boredom breaks
  (a wedding: flecks of rice) flecks
   on windowpanes where
  a branchlet taps (a witch's claw)
   rust red in rain now
   O lovely failing of the light
that opens our pupils as sunlight never does
   admitting

pale sun   brown lawn   blurred hills   dull sky
  this the necessary palette
   bare bones of our time here
   where all days are Sundays
  disguised as work days

SUNDAY RAIN

The window screen
is trying to do
its crossword puzzle
but appears to know
only vertical words.

PHENOMENA

The tide goes up and down in the creek.
I wake each morning to witness
the black-clay banks bared like senile gums
or the marsh eclipsed by a second sky.

My furnace went out.
The man who fixed it let me look
at the rejuvenated flame;
it was astonishing.
In a cave of asbestos a vivid elf
went *dancy, dancy, dancy;*
his fingers and feet were uncountable;
he was all hot eye
and merry, so merry he roared.

I handle stones.
They like, perhaps, being handled.
In the earth, at the shovel's first strike,
they are mysterious—one might be
the tip of a China-sized cathedral.
But grubbing and cunning and cursing
bring them one by one to light,
disappointing when dried in the sun,
yet *there*, waterproof, fireproof,
dull veins disclosing a logic of form
and formation, but endurance the foremost quality.
I pile them, alter their position in the universe;
by a tissue's-width difference, it matters.
Their surfaces say something to my hands.

At night, lying down, I cannot breathe.
A tree inside me clenches and I sweat.
There are reasons, there is medicine;
the frost of death
has found a chink in me, is all.
I breathe easier and, breathing, sleep.
The tide sighs and rises in my sleep.
The flame is furious in its cell below.
Under the moon the cold stones wait.

BOIL

In the night the white skin
cries aloud to be broken,
but finds itself a cruel prison;
so it is with reason,
which holds the terror in,
undoubted though the infection.

MIME

on the black stage he
was in an imaginary box
mime mime mime mime mi

its inner surface stopped his
hand.   the audience gasped
amazing amazing amazing ama

he climbed stairs that were
not there, walked and went
nowhere nowhere nowhere now

the real world was what his
head told his hands to delimit
in air in air in air in a

chill certain as glass.   the
other world was fuzzy and
treacherous treacherous trea

he took a plane, it began
to fall, the passengers shrieked
help o God o help help he

the mime imagined a box.
his feet hit glass, the plane's
fall halted.   up, up.   praise be
mimesis mimesis mimesis mime

NOTE TO THE PREVIOUS
TENANTS

Thank you for leaving the bar of soap,
the roll of paper towels,
the sponge mop, the bucket.

I tried to scrub the white floor clean,
discovered it impossible,
and realized you had tried too.

Often, no doubt. The long hair in the sink
was a clue to what? Were you
boys or girls or what?

How often did you dance on the floor?
The place was broom clean. Your lives
were a great wind that has swept by.

Thank you; even the dirt
seemed a gift, a continuity
underlying the breaking of leases.

And the soap, green in veins
like meltable marble, and curved
like a bit of an ideal woman.

Lone, I took a bath with your soap
and had no towel not paper ones
and dried in the air like the floor.

DUTCH CLEANSER

My grandmother used it, Dutch Cleanser,
in the dark Shillington house,
in the kitchen darkened by the grape arbor,
and I was frightened of the lady on the can.
Why was she carrying a stick?
Why couldn't we see her face?

Now, an aging modern man,
estranged, alone, and medium gray,
I tip Dutch Cleanser onto a sponge,
here in this narrow bathroom,
where the ventilator fan has to rumble
when all I want to switch on is light.

The years have spilled since Shillington,
the daily *Eagle*s stacked in the closet
have burst the roof! Look up,
Deutsche Grossmutter—I am here!
You have changed, I have changed,
Dutch Cleanser has changed not at all.

The lady is still upholding the stick
chasing dirt, and her face
is so angry we dare not see it.
The dirt she is chasing is ahead of her,
around the can, like a minute hand
the hour hand pushes around.

HEADING FOR NANDI

Out of Honolulu
heading for Nandi
I ask them, "Where's Nandi?"
The man tells me, "Fiji."

The airport is open
the night sky black panels
between cement pillars.
I wish I had a woman.

Around me Australians
are holding hands matily
as back in Waikiki
the honeymooners strolled.

By daylight bikinis
strolled bare on the pavement
the honeymoon brides
with waists white as milk

and the Japanese couples
posed each for the other
the women as dainty
as self-painted dolls

and the watching Polynesians
laughed quick as Fayaway
dark as cooking chocolate
that always tasted bitter

and the haunted Americans
with flatland accents
in plastic leis wandered
the blue streets of love.

From the taxi I saw
two men embracing
embracing and crying.
I assumed they were sailors.

Nandi? I'll see it
or die in these hours
that face me like panels
in a chapel by Rothko.

I wish I had a woman
to touch me or tell me
she is frightened to go there
or would be, but for me.

A Note About the Author

JOHN UPDIKE *was born in 1932 in Shillington, Pennsylvania. He graduated* summa cum laude *from Harvard in 1954, and spent a year in England on the Knox Fellowship, at the Ruskin School of Drawing and Fine Art in Oxford. From 1955 to 1957 he was a member of the staff of* The New Yorker, *to which he has contributed short stories, poems, parodies, and criticism. His own books include eight novels, five short-story collections, four volumes of poetry, two of criticism, and a play*, Buchanan Dying. *Mr. Updike presently lives in Massachusetts.*

A Note on the Type

The text of this book was set on the Linotype in Janson, a recutting made directly from type cast from matrices long thought to have been made by the Dutchman Anton Janson, who was a practicing type founder in Leipzig during the years 1668–87. However, it has been conclusively demonstrated that these types are actually the work of Nicholas Kis (1650–1702), a Hungarian, who most probably learned his trade from the Dutch type founder Dirk Voskens. The type is an excellent example of the influential and sturdy Dutch types that prevailed in England up to the time William Caslon developed his own incomparable designs from them.

Composed, printed, and bound by American Book–Stratford Press, Saddle Brook, New Jersey